Burning Down the Business

A Cautionary Tale

of

Business Acquisition

Larry A Forsythe

DEDICATION

Dedicated to my sweetheart, enduring privations because she loves me instead of someone with more sense. I love you, dearest. Thank you for staying. Heaven knows why you haven't left me.

CONTENTS

ACKNOWLEDGMENTS

To every business acquisition guru who encouraged us to believe their training was what we needed to make a mint buying businesses... Thanks for the disaster.

1 INTRODUCTION

Dear Reader,

Have you been listening to gurus who say you can make a mint in just a few years by buying businesses? We're a real life lesson, but our story isn't what the gurus tell you.

You couldn't make up a story like ours. Even so, we have to fictionalise a bit. There would be hell to pay if we didn't and a mountain of money is already demanded by people who didn't get defrauded half as badly as we have been. Obviously, the names in our story and a few details are changed. We're supposed to say that's to protect the innocent, but it's really mostly to duck out of showing ourselves as the suckers we are. We promise our fictions simplify what happened instead of embellishing on it. By the time you finish our sorry tale, you may not believe that. Unfortunately it's true.

Put fools in front of a malignant cheater, and this is what happens – burning down the business and all the lives it touches.

Welcome to our nightmare.

May you never have one like it.

Regards,

Lawrence (Larry) A Forsythe

2 CORKY FINDS A TARGET

My best bud Corky Widdershins, our friend Mo Hapliss and I were looking for businesses to acquire. The gurus say it's possible to buy a business without needing to put in much cash and build up to having a million in the bank within as little as three years. We thought a lot of what they said wouldn't really pan out, but a million within twice as long would be fine. A million *ever* would be fine. We hadn't explicitly decided to go into it together, but we got along well and thought we could be a good team if the cards fell right.

There are plenty of ways to find a business to buy, including business brokers and online markets that specialise in companies for sale. General online markets like eBuyNow (not its real name, of course) where you normally buy shoes, toys, and other such stuff aren't meant for selling a company. That's where Corky found Garden Living Space Ltd. It should have been our first red flag.

 Remember, I'm changing some details here. As of this writing, there is no such company as Garden Living Space Ltd. There are no websites at gardenls.com or gardenlivingspace.co.uk or gardenlistingspace.com.

Corky met with Peter and Fanny Broadtail. All three of them were sales orientated personalities, so they got on like a house afire.

The Broadtails wanted to sell their business and Corky wanted to sell them on himself as the buyer. They had an easy job meeting with him. They weren't just keen to sell, they had spent their careers selling. Corky was a wannabe at sales. He can talk a mile a minute and sound good about the pitch, but his actual work experience is all over the place and doesn't include being a master at selling.

The Broadtails said they resorted to eBuyNow because they felt business brokers wouldn't be worth their commissions. They knew how to sell goods, so they could sell the company themselves. How hard could it be?

They convinced Corky that Garden Living Space was a great business for generating free cash flow. The corporation's annual turnover was £3.7 million. It was small enough to wrap hands around and big enough to support their self-indulgent lifestyle. It was essentially a sales and marketing machine, they said. The delivery work, primarily building or upgrading garden offices and garden rooms, was done by contract labour so only a handful of people were on payroll.

Corky was the only one of us who had actually acquired a small business already. It was a fish and chips takeaway shop. He got it for the princely sum of one pound sterling and it went under in less than two years. He told me lots of reasons why the failure wasn't his fault, and of course nobody sells a business for £1 unless it has a heap of trouble, but still... How does anybody fail with a chippy in jolly old England?

Anyway, Corky couldn't buy GLS on his own because the chippy failure left him in the midst of a period being banned from serving as a company director, not to mention in debt up to his ears. That's where I came in to help my bestie, and then Mo.

 Finding a business is up for sale through non-standard avenues should have made us more wary, and perhaps the only one of us with a business failure to his name shouldn't have been the first to judge whether or not it was a good bet.

3 STOP AND GO AND STOP

Corky recruited me into the deal. He had found this great opportunity. The company sold based on high quality, not low price. Its target market was affluent pensioners willing to splash out on top grade garden rooms instead of settling for poor quality to keep the price down. It was just the right size to take care of both of us financially for as long as we might want, and we would be working together.

Spend the work week with my best mate and not have to worry about money any more? Sign me up!

If the financial sector ran on fancy spreadsheets, I would be in the City of London making moolah hand over fist. The financial sector wants people to think it's based on cold hard data. After the crash in the late Noughties, most people have figured out it runs on something else, a twisted magic that bundles up bad investments so they look good, invents fortunes or catastrophes out of thin air, and seduces people into parting with their cash for mirages.

I do elaborate maths, which I love, for projects that pay peanuts. I have even more kids than Corky does, from even more ex-wives. They eat whatever money I make, plus some. I love them all dearly and try not to get upset about living in penury to take care of them. My sweetheart puts up with it all, bless her, and Corky's puts up with him.

I don't have any more money than Corky and I've got a bigger pile of bills to pay, but nothing bars me from being a director of a company. Corky couldn't very well acquire a company he wasn't allowed to direct, so he needed someone who could do that. We also thought my mathematical analysis would set the price right and convince somebody to lend us money to buy the business. Surely my rock solid numbers would do the trick.

We missed the memo about the financial sector's twisted magic. I haven't been to the financial version of wizard school. I had a silly notion that we just needed for me to look up formulas, plug them together into an analysis, and show them to money people. Acquisition funding would spill out, we'd buy GLS and we'd be set for life.

I built financial analysis and projections for GLS. They were impressive, or at least I thought they were. They churned out valuation, cash flow projections and deal structure analysis based on published formulas from acquisition gurus. We were ready to make a deal.

That's when Peter Broadtail died. This was before the COVID pandemic, so death wasn't a drawn-out ordeal in a hospital ICU. One moment the Broadtails were chatting over dinner. The next moment he stopped in mid-sentence, went goggle-eyed and pitched face first into the pasta. Boom! Massive stroke, apparently. You never know when your time will run out.

Fanny invited Corky and me to the funeral. We went. It was weird, going to the funeral of someone we had barely met. Fanny wasn't up to discussing the deal for months after that.

It was understandable. She must be grieving. They had been a team and now she had to do all the bossing they used to do together, or at least that's what we believed was happening. It was the latter part of high season for the business, too. In the warm season of the year, keeping up with the pace of sales orders was an all hands, all the time affair.

Fanny called Corky again in the seasons of dark, cold and wet. Orders fall off then. Soon after Peter died, she hired a General Manager to help her run the business. From the way she described him, Richard Little practically hung the moon. He knew the industry inside and out, had loads of useful contacts, had skills upon skills, and was fantastic at running the business. Fanny hardly had to lift a finger any more.

This made the business an even better buy. Dick, the new key management, would stay with the company. That's supposed to make the transition smoother for new owners, whereas before we would have been learning it all from the Broadtails and taking over all the hands-on management ourselves.

After I updated my analysis with financial figures from the past few months, Corky and I took my numbers to money people. We couldn't find a lender willing to provide anywhere near enough funding for the price Fanny wanted.

We invited Mo into the deal. Mo had greased the wheels for a previous acquisition attempt at another business, finding the funding we needed. The earlier deal collapsed because Corky and I missed an essential item in our due diligence. The money people noticed, got spooked and withdrew.

Mo had a better personal credit rating thanks to some illiquid assets but not much cash, a better backstory and CV, was married without any kids to support, and seemed to be able to get people to trust him. He couldn't spin a lie very well at all. Maybe that was why people trusted him.

Mo took my numbers to money people. He could get pretty close to the funding we needed, but not quite all the way there. To land the deal, we needed Fanny to agree to more of a stretch on the deferred portion of what we would pay her. She refused to flex, so the deal was off again.

 I think the financial sector has a warped view of risk, but we should have paid more attention to their reluctance about funding acquisition of GLS. We also should have paid a lot more attention to Fanny's unwillingness to compromise.

4 BACK AROUND AGAIN

The COVID-19 pandemic arrived. We thanked our lucky stars that we were not taking over a business just as the whole world went into lockdown. Our respective households focused on trying not to catch the terrifying virus. GLS was the last thing on our minds.

In the autumn Fanny called Corky. She said that after a couple of months of shutdown, her wonderful GM Dick came up with ways to carry on doing business despite the pandemic. With him, she had cut costs, streamlined procedures, consolidated the premises from an office and a high bay mini-warehouse to only the office, and made all sorts of changes. Although revenue had taken a hit and was running just under half the pace it had been pre-pandemic, the business was more efficient than ever now.

Would we be interested in buying 70% of the shares for less than half her previous price, on the condition that we had to pay it all up front?

What if the business could lend us the money to pay her for the purchase?

A self-funded acquisition is a business buyer's dream, especially for people like us who have perennially empty wallets. We would still need to cover acquisition costs, but Corky wrangled a loan from the Coronavirus Business Interruption Loan Scheme into a company we had formed to use as an acquisition vehicle for the earlier deal that fell through. CBILS loans had no personal guarantee unless they were whoppers, which ours wasn't, and we could use the money to grow the business pretty much any way we wanted. The legal costs to acquire a bigger business certainly qualified as an effort to grow our empty acquisition company Varzan Limited. We had £50k in hand, enough to cover the cost of due diligence and legal work.

We didn't need Mo to bring in funding any more, but after all the work he put in trying to line up funding for us twice before, it felt like we ought to offer to include him. Having lost clients for his business in the pandemic and in need of new revenue, he said yes to our invitation.

Mo was better at reading contracts and talking with solicitors than we were. That's how we divided the duties. He would work with solicitors on the legal paperwork through deal completion, including any last minute negotiation about details. Corky and I would operate the business after acquisition.

We all met with Fanny and Dick for one last sanity check. Fanny seemed recovered from Peter's death. Dick sounded like he knew what he was doing. He was willing to stay at the same salary with a couple of adjustments. He wanted his bonus turned into contributions to his pension in order to reduce his taxes. He also wanted his company car arrangement changed so it didn't cost so much in tax on company benefits. We verbally agreed to that.

 We thought acquiring the remaining 30% of shares was the deferred portion of the acquisition, so we weren't paying for the entire acquisition up front. But we were paying for 70% up front. That was dumb. We should have paid for 30% to no more than 50% up front. The rest of the 70% should have been delayed a few months, released only after contingencies were met, and subject to deductions for breaches of acquisition warranties. That would have given us leverage in case we needed it.

5 WRINKLES

Wrinkles are to be expected. At first they were nothing to get agitated about.

Dick flip-flopped about exactly how he wanted to get his bonus. Instead of having it paid into his pension, he'd like to get some equity in the company, maybe 5% to 10% of the shares. Then he would get dividends instead of a bonus. Or maybe he would like to get bonus payments the way he currently got them. Or maybe he could get both equity and bonus? Mo quashed that. No double dipping.

We had no idea how important it was that Dick didn't end up with any shares.

For the company car, a government incentive made an electric vehicle the best way to drop the benefits tax. Dick said electric wouldn't do. He had to drive all over the country and couldn't spend large chunks of his workdays recharging it. Maybe he could have a plug-in hybrid instead. But he didn't like the tax rate on that, so maybe an electric would do after all – one that had lots of range. It had to make the right impression. A Nissan Leaf wouldn't do. BMW, or Audi, or how about Tesla, or an electric Range Rover? This wouldn't do, that wouldn't do... Mo went back and forth with Dick's indecision and strove to rein in his escalating desires.

Company cars were a shared obsession for Dick and Fanny, each of whom drove one. Fanny had bizarre expectations about GLS continuing to let her drive the Audi, insuring it and covering some other costs for it. She didn't want to accept that a company car belonged to the company and was part of the asset she was selling. Mo had to talk her around from that. Somehow at the end of all that bickering our deal price crept up from money funded out of GLS to also eat some of our CBILS loan. We no longer had enough money for acquisition costs. Too much was going to Fanny.

Corky and I didn't have an established link with any law firms. We couldn't very well start off with a solicitor we didn't know by admitting we didn't have enough money to pay the roughly £30k they would charge for our acquisition legals. We needed a solicitor willing to defer payment until we had access to the GLS bank account.

Felix Fairweather of Nunely, Fairweather, Morris & Associates had worked on a couple of other ventures for Mo, so Mo got him to sign on as our solicitor. Fairweather agreed not to bill his usual up-front retainer, instead sending us a bill for the whole job at deal completion on Net 14 Days terms. We would pay him out of GLS after the acquisition. Mo asked what would happen if the deal fell apart. Fairweather said in that case we would have to pay him out of our own funds. We were certain the deal was going to be great, so we didn't worry about the what-if that surely wouldn't happen.

Liam Cadfellow was Fanny's solicitor. When we looked him up online, his specialty was real estate, not business, let alone mergers and acquisitions. Fanny's accountant was Max Minford Accountants Ltd. We didn't have one yet.

It was time for due diligence and legal bickering to commence on parallel tracks. That's when things began to go squirrelly.

 We got into a situation where we had to complete the deal. Backing out wasn't an option. We should never have allowed ourselves to get into a position with no escape hatch.

6 DUE DILIGENCE

We no longer had enough money to hire professional help for due diligence, either. After some dithering, we arranged to go to the GLS office and spend a few days going through everything ourselves. We chose a date when Mo had a schedule conflict and couldn't participate. Aware of how our previous deal fell apart over our omission in due diligence, he warned us to be careful and thorough this time. We swore we would.

Corky and I had a great time at GLS. We got acquainted with the handful of office and field staff who were on payroll. The office staff were women handling marketing, sales, coordination of the contractors who did the sales visits to prospects and builders who did actual work at customers' homes, and administrative duties. The field staff were a couple of guys who drove around in company vans doing small jobs. They could redo sealants and do any work under the GLS ten year guarantee that didn't require the skillset and tools (and cost) of calling out the builders. We noticed they all hated their bosses Fanny and Dick, but a lot of workers hate management, so we didn't worry about it. We hobnobbed with Fanny and Dick. We asked for all sorts of files and looked through what they gave us.

Unfortunately, we didn't get anywhere near everything we asked for. Fanny said Peter handled those things before his death and kept all the documents in a super-secure computer server. When he died, access to it was locked. The IT service managing the server refused to allow anyone into it, including her.

The files involved included employment contracts, policy documents, procedures, vendor agreements... nearly everything important other than bank statements and accounting reports. Across nearly a year and a half since Peter's death, Fanny and Dick had not lifted a finger to reinstate any of it. There were no replacements or updates for contracts or documents except insurance policies that had renewed since Peter died. We got the impression that was a matter of sheer laziness, being happy to keep on doing what they had been doing without bothering to replace missing paperwork. Fanny and Dick seemed friendly, apologetic about how much was missing, and happily looking forward to deal completion. The staff seemed hopeful about us becoming their new bosses.

We felt uneasy, but determined to make the acquisition. We hadn't seen any smoking guns and we had no idea how we would repay our CBILS loans if we had to pay Fairweather's bill without getting a productive business acquisition from all this effort.

 We had failed at due diligence before. We should have hired a professional for it this time and should not have gone ahead with the deal if we couldn't. We should have at least been smart enough not to go ahead with the deal unless we got all the information we needed for due diligence.

7 LEGALS COMMENCE

With hardly any notice, Fanny left the UK to spend Christmas and see in the New Year at a second home in France, which she bought after Peter died in anticipation of retirement. She said spending holidays in the house she had shared with Peter would hurt too much. She had done it once and wouldn't do it again. She would be back in a couple of weeks.

Within a few days, escalating pandemic cases prompted the borders to close. Fanny wouldn't be able to return for months. Mo remarked he wouldn't be surprised if she never returned.

Cadfellow and Fairweather divided responsibility for acquisition paperwork and started writing first drafts. Mo started marking up the drafts. But Fanny stayed in the middle of the loop, refusing to allow the solicitors to talk with each other directly. To make matters worse, she said Minford was researching exactly how to structure the transaction.

Nobody could write that part of the paperwork until Minford revealed the proper structure.

Weeks passed in increasing frustration. Our engagement with Fairweather was fixed cost up to a date that allowed for some slippage in the deal, but such prolonged vagueness about the transaction structure put us near, then at, then past the date when the fixed cost expired. Our legal costs were going up.

Eventually Fanny provided contact information for Cadfellow and granted permission for the solicitors to collaborate directly instead of through her.

Then Minford came through with the transaction structure, which was relayed to us through Cadfellow. We had understood earlier that GLS, like us, took out a CBILS loan. We could see it in the financial reports and bank statements. It was for precisely the threshold beyond which Fanny would have been required to sign a personal guarantee.

It was the money Minford now said should be loaned from GLS to our acquisition company Varzan and then paid by Varzan to Fanny for the acquisition. Fanny had drained out everything else except about £100k in operating capital, the minimum amount of operating capital we insisted had to be in the bank account after the acquisition completed.

Fairweather and Mo questioned this and especially questioned how repayment of the CBILS loan and the acquisition loan could be done with this structure. Minford outlined a complicated path for repayments, but we didn't understand it and wondered whether it was right.

 It may seem like we should have recognised this arrangement as wrong, but it wasn't anywhere near as bad as what some British business magnates have done. We should have known that's for the elite making big deals, people whose names begin with 'Sir', not for Lilliputians like us.

Having noticed that Minford charged an arm and a leg, we intended to switch to a different accountant after the acquisition, and have the same accountant handle both GLS and Varzan. Corky and I, having no real business happening in Varzan yet, hadn't lined up an accountant. Mo suggested using his accountant Stella Franks. We could begin by asking Franks for a sanity check about the loan repayment flow. We agreed.

In retrospect, Mo should have drawn Franks the whole picture as soon as she agreed to take us on as a new client. At the time, we all thought the weeks of delay from Minford had been taken up by professional research into the proper way to structure the acquisition transaction. Mo told Franks about Varzan borrowing from GLS and adding money from its CBILS loan to pay Fanny for 70% of the equity. He mentioned that GLS owed money elsewhere, but didn't make the source of the loan from GLS to Varzan explicitly clear. Mo was focused on the mechanics of loan repayments, which nobody realised was a mistake.

Franks said to draw up the acquisition legals so that each month, GLS would pay Varzan as its main owner enough out of its profits to cover the loan payments. Then Varzan should split that money to make its own CBILS loan payment and make a payment to GLS on its acquisition loan. After that, GLS should use the payment it got from Varzan to make the payment it owed on its external loan. It seemed silly, making a bunch of money travel around a loop, but all these transactions needed to show up in the financial books. If the money didn't make a loop through Varzan, technically Varzan wouldn't be regarded as paying down its debt to GLS.

It made everyone's head spin. I literally had to draw a flow diagram to make sense of it. Everyone else asked for a copy of the diagram.

 When something seems weird, especially to the professionals, maybe it really is weird. Maybe it's too weird to accept. Also, when asking a professional for advice, we should have laid out the whole context instead of only a piece of it. If Franks had known the entire picture, she might have told us to stop.

8 SIGNS OF SOMETHING LURKING

Mo began to grumble about a disturbing pattern in changes Fanny was demanding through Cadfellow in the acquisition legals. Mo said she was inserting clauses to evade responsibility for something, most likely overdue bills, but he couldn't be sure what it was.

We debated what to do and consulted Fairweather. A huge bundle of disclosure documents was overdue to be in our hands. The legals still included a wide range of acquisition warranties: equipment in serviceable condition, compliance with regulations, no overdue bills over a specified size and age, no unpaid taxes, no outstanding customer complaints, no litigation, no threats of legal action against GLS...

Fairweather said if we did not find anything too awful in the disclosure bundle, those warranties should protect us against most undisclosed skeletons in the GLS closet. We decided that left relatively small, recent unpaid bills as the main risk. Fanny was evading responsibility for bills under £2100 (a peculiar amount) and more than six weeks old, but allowed us to claim for unpaid bills above that amount if they totalled more than £8000. In a company with annual revenue that was still more than £1.6 million, surely we could cope with such limited exposure.

We knew some of the warranties were fiction. By accident, Corky stumbled into an online news article about arrest and conviction of one of the office staff on a drug-related charge. The warranties said none of the employees had a criminal record. We discussed what to do about the employee and decided to keep our mouths shut, monitor her work and avoid giving her financial duties. We didn't find anything similar about the rest of the staff. We should have looked harder.

 To our surprise, the druggie later turned out to be one of the most energetic, productive and reliable GLS employees. However, we were too quick to shrug off the fact that Fanny willingly lied in a business contract about whether any of the employees had a problematic past. Were there any other personnel problems? How many other lies did she tell us and how serious were they?

Really, we talked ourselves into continuing. If we backed out of the deal now, we would have to pay most of our CBILS loan of £50k in Varzan to Fairweather and have nothing to show for it. We would not have enough left to do something else to raise revenue and start paying off that loan in a few months. In essence, we allowed a few thousand pounds of tail to wag us as the dog.

Mo was also deep into wrangling about the shareholders' agreement that would take effect from the moment of the acquisition. We had no quibble with Fanny's desire for her shares to get dividends on the same proportional basis as ours, but she wanted to force us to buy her remaining 30% sooner than we might want and at a higher valuation. Negotiations about that took an immense amount of Mo's time and attention, and it ran up our legal bill even more.

 Somewhere in that bunch of haggling, Mo got one change that would later turn out to be terribly important for us. He got Fanny to agree that her remaining 30% of the shares would be non-voting. We made many blunders, but we got this right. Fanny would have no say in how we handled the business after deal completion.

The disclosure bundle arrived. It was an enormous digital pile of document scans and other files. Corky and I (mostly me) started wading through it, looking for any of the many things we couldn't get our hands on in due diligence and any signs of the types of trouble the acquisition warranties pledged we wouldn't have. Even with the disclosure bundle, we still had a lot of gaps in the due diligence checklist we had gotten from gurus. We asked for documents to fill those gaps. At first Fanny continued her story that she couldn't access them either, but then we asked for a few documents she should have and she simply refused.

As we approached the expected completion date, Fanny announced that due to the usual seasonal drop in business in deep winter, the bank account wouldn't contain at least the requisite £100,000 when the acquisition occurred. She wanted us to credit thousands in expected revenue toward that balance without counting bills that would come due in the same post-deal interval.

After a few rounds clashing about that, Mo gave Fairweather a few alternatives and told him that if Fanny wouldn't accept any of them, the deal was off. Maybe he should have done that about other disconcerting parts of the deal, too. Faced with that ultimatum, Fanny agreed the amount we had to pay at deal completion would be adjusted down by the amount of the shortfall in the bank account so GLS would have £100K in cash when we took over, even if some of it was CBILS money.

Trying to wade through all of this to finalise the deal before legal costs swamped us kept us running so fast in our hamster wheel, we didn't stop to think hard enough about the picture that was taking shape and whether we should back away. Also, did I mention that we should have insisted on getting all the materials needed for due diligence? And that the disclosure bundle should have filled any gaps left in due diligence?

9 ACQUISITION AT LAST

We got to deal completion on the last Thursday in February. One of us had to be physically at the office on Deal Day. How could the staff take us seriously as new owners if none of us were there for the transition?

Unlike many businesses, the handful of office employees at GLS worked at the office, not from home. They were careful about pandemic restrictions in the rest of their lives. They didn't wear face masks or distance from each other in the office, behaving as though they were a family 'bubble' in a home.

Corky and I, who were supposed to be the ones to handle day to day operations, couldn't go. Corky's mum was in hospital with serious heart trouble. (She ended up getting a stent.) I had a contract with a big multinational company to build a mathematical model for something I couldn't talk about with anyone else, not that anybody would have understood if I tried. That client is paranoid about anyone learning their trade secrets, so I'm not allowed to say who I was working for. I call them World Class Eggheads (Eggheads for short). They had a major executive meeting scheduled about their initiative. They insisted I had to slave away full time on their maths to get as much done as possible before the meeting, then be on hand to answer questions about the halfway-complete model's capabilities so far and what still had to be added. I was unavailable to be on-site at GLS until the second Monday after Deal Day. I didn't dare quit the Eggheads until after GLS started paying me enough wages and dividends to make up for losing that income.

In my next life maybe I shouldn't have so many kids, but the need to take care of them kept me from ditching that contract, thank heaven.

Mo went, even though he was the only one of the three of us who would not be on payroll due to not normally having an operational role. He insisted on wearing a face mask in the office. Mo's wife worked at a GP surgery. She got potential virus exposure every day, but she was obsessive about masks and hygiene and social distancing. Mo stayed home as much as possible. Mo said they were both more vulnerable than most if they caught the virus. They ordered groceries delivered and generally would only visit with people outdoors with plenty of distance. He wasn't keen to take chances, but he was at GLS on Deal Day. He said the staff took his mask-wearing in stride.

At long last Fairweather and Cadfellow waved their magic legal wands and we got control of GLS... sort of. GLS was ours, or at least mostly ours, for better or for worse.

 We intended to meet with the sales team and builders as soon as possible after deal completion. They were contractors, not employees, but they were crucial to the business. They're people, as much in need of human niceties as anyone else. It took us weeks to get around to those meetings. The sales reps in particular might have been less grumbly about changes we had to make if we had met with them face to face immediately.

10 GETTING INTO ACCOUNTS AND BILLS

As the new Managing Director, I got access to the bank account. Notice I didn't say I got control of it, and it wasn't exactly me who got access because the two-factor authentication gadget arrived at the GLS office on Deal Day. Mo got access, masquerading as me until I could go to the office. I'm not eager to get sued for discussing what that high street bank would soon do to us, so I call them Big Money Bank plc (BMB).

In post-Brexit Britain, BMB could not tell us a procedure for processing a bank mandate to give me full control of the account unless Fanny could walk into a British branch herself to do her part of it. They had branches in France, but even if one had been near her, French branches were no longer entitled to do anything about UK accounts.

BMB seemed to make up a procedure as they went along. First they had Fanny add me as a user, but she was only allowed to add me as a secondary user with limited capabilities due to not having a bank mandate in place to change the all-powerful primary user. I could see statements and transactions. I could pay bills. The account could take incoming bank transfers. I couldn't do much else. Or rather, that's the situation Mo found, logging in as me.

 The legals should (and did) specify that control of all sorts of things would be transferred at deal completion. Keys to the office and company vehicles. Control of the bank account and accounting system. Yadda yadda yadda. Fanny no longer had votes, but she was the only person in control of the money!

Dick was out doing whatever he did as General Manager, which didn't include being in the office much. The field staff were out doing small jobs at customer sites. After pleasantries and a quick round of cheers about deal completion, with cake of course, Mo asked the office staff for any bills that urgently needed to be paid. In light of the legal clauses that bothered him, Mo thought he should look for overdue bills first.

Toni brought a stack of paper bills. For the first few days, Toni kept bringing in bills one or two at a time, always on paper. At last Mo asked her to please scan them and send them to his Varzan email address until we could set up something more proper.

It turned out that most bills came in electronically through email and Fanny made Toni print them all on paper for her inbox, although she must have gotten them by email after she went to France. Toni seemed relieved stop all that printing.

Some of the bills were due soon. A bunch were overdue. In that first tranche, they were due recently enough and for small enough amounts to scoot below the criteria Fanny had insisted upon for us to be able to claim acquisition warranty breaches. We shrugged. We expected some of that. Mo started keeping track of them in a spreadsheet. We didn't have access to the online accounting system yet.

 Everything was supposed to be handed over at deal completion: control of the bank account, the office, company vehicles, service provider accounts, authorisation codes at Companies House and HMRC... everything. We didn't even have the smarts to get or compile a comprehensive list of all of that ahead of the transaction. We wouldn't get full control of the bank account for a month and a half, and that was only the tip of the iceberg. We had held nothing back from the purchase price. We had to forge ahead, doing what we could with what we had and dealing with each item as we discovered it, because once again we had left ourselves no leverage and no escape hatch.

Within a couple of days, Mo's Varzan email account was swimming in email attachments that contained bills. GLS didn't have permission-controlled shared digital storage. It kept photos from customer jobs on an in-house server, some files in a cloud-based storage account, a mishmash... We had a Microsoft 365® account for Varzan. Mo created a folder tree there for managing bills. As he got them, he put them in the Unpaid folder. He moved them to Scheduled when he had set up a payment from the bank account, and to Paid when the payment had gone out. He couldn't enter them into the accounting system because Minford controlled that and had not granted us a login for it yet.

11 RESURRECTING THE MARKETING

As soon as Mo thought (an important word) he had paid the most pressing bills, he met with Lisa about marketing. This was Mo's weakest skill area – to be honest, he was incompetent at marketing and sales, and he knew it. Corky said it couldn't wait until he could get to the office. In the disclosure bundle, Corky noticed that Fanny's reduction of marketing spend in the past several months had become an almost complete cut-off, timed so we would not see it yet in financial statements available for our due diligence visit. If we did no marketing, we would make no sales, have no revenue and quickly collapse.

We wanted Corky to be our Chief Operating Officer. He was the most salesy of us, so we intended to have him be in charge of operations including marketing and sales, but we didn't dare wait. Corky said most people had to see ads several times over a stretched-out period before they would schedule a visit from a sales representative. It would take three months for an increase in advertising to fully come through in sales figures. Mo had to restart advertising right away.

Lisa told Mo that an average of 30 new leads should be waiting for attention on Monday mornings. In peak season, it would be around 50. In the depths of December and early January, that might drop off to 8 or 10, but by late February it should be around 20. Our first Monday in charge, when Mo met with Lisa, we had three.

Not being any good at marketing himself, Mo asked Lisa which advertising would be quickest to produce new sales at a reasonable cost. She recommended a particular national print media package that was expensive and a less costly package that involved print outlets the next level down, major regional and local publications. These two packages, especially the national one, had provided the most leads for GLS in the past. Mo gulped and asked a couple of questions about the expensive national package, then told her to negotiate as low a restart price as possible and bring that to him for a decision. He also told her to monitor performance of ads closely. We could only afford ads that produced sales.

From home, Corky started looking at whether we wanted to modify any of the adverts before they ran, but he only had a little time here and there. Although the pandemic kept him from being with his mum while she was in hospital, the family emergency caused a flurry of urgent errands and shuttling of children back and forth. With the Eggheads demanding full-time hours from me, I didn't have time for more than a glance, either. The adverts worked well enough before Fanny cut them off, so we hoped they would work well enough again.

 Our Heads of Terms offering to acquire the business should have included a clause requiring Fanny to continue operating in the usual way up to deal completion. Not having that clause allowed her to stop advertising, killing momentum and leaving us to resurrect it with a lag of months before we could hope for anything resembling normal sales and revenue.

12 MORE BILLS

Mo went back to the stack of bills. Rent was due that Monday. The stack of bills included a demand for unpaid rent and an unsigned rent review from June that raised the rent about 25%. He dug the lease out of our due diligence files and called the landlord, where he spoke with Janet Jones whose name appeared on nearly everything about renting the office.

The lease did allow the landlord to conduct a rent review at that point, three years into a five year lease. It allowed the rent to be raised with no cap on the increase. Jones produced a long chain of email messages between herself and Fanny about it. Fanny's messages made it clear that she acknowledged the rent increase even though she never signed the formal documentation.

Fanny simply never paid the increase. She continued paying the old rent rate, building up arrears. The bill for back rent was significantly higher than that could explain, which left Mo confused. He dug into our due diligence files again.

Early in the pandemic when Fanny shut down the business for a few weeks to figure out what to do, she didn't pay rent at all. A few landlords waived some of their rent during that period. The most generous example any of us personally knew about was a little shop in my town where the wealthy landlady told the shop to skip the rent for six months, pay half rent for the next six months, and never make it up to her. Hopeful, Mo asked Jones whether GLS had gotten rent abeyance for the months when Fanny paid nothing. We didn't hope for anything like the little shop near me, but we hoped for something. Nope. Fanny simply withheld a couple of months of rent. GLS owed those months plus the shortfall since July.

Jones offered to waive penalties and interest. Mo looked at how much he shelled out for overdue bills in just a few days, other bills coming due soon, and the whopping bills Lisa was about to incur (the national package wanted £25k per month for at least a 3 month commitment)... and somehow Mo pleaded Jones into giving us a payment schedule that stretched out our catch-up on the rent over the next couple of months.

Next, Mo found utility bills, which were up to date but astoundingly high. When the fixed rate tariffs for electricity and natural gas expired, Fanny had let them revert to the standard variable tariff, which is always the most expensive rate a company offers. When Mo tried to sign us up on a fixed rate, he was told that had to be done by Peter as the account contact. Mo explained that the company had changed hands, and was told to have Peter provide his consent to transfer control of the accounts. Mo had a maddening time getting the utility company to understand that we couldn't get Peter's consent from the grave. It took Mo about a week and a half of letters and phone calls to get our utility accounts squared away.

We went through the same thing getting control of GLS accounts at a number of other suppliers. Fanny had never bothered to get control of the accounts after Peter died.

 It's basic to make sure the person selling anything to you has the right to sell it. Fanny had the right to sell GLS. But in light of Peter's death, we should have checked whether she had the right and capability to transfer control of all the pieces of GLS. She mostly didn't. The only account where she bothered to make sure of getting complete control after his death was the bank account.

During our first couple of days in the business, Mo gave Kath letters to send to all the suppliers and current customers about the change of management. She led the sales team and collaborated with Toni on scheduling 'fittings'

(installations and builds at customer sites), so it seemed like she would generally be recognisable to most people we needed to notify. Most of our notice letters went out by email from her account. A few had to be sent by post.

 In the coming weeks, we would learn the hard way that GLS did not have a complete list of suppliers, had never gotten control of most supplier accounts updated after Peter died, and did not have adequate records about its customers and what it had done for each of them. There weren't any acquisition warranties about any of that in our deal.

13 VANS NO GO

The two maintenance guys were supposed to each drive a transit van, running around doing small jobs where it wasn't cost effective to bring in the builders (about some of them, I use that term loosely) who put in the bespoke garden rooms we sold. The first week we had the business, Mo never saw Vince or Pat. They usually went out before the office opened and got back after the office closed for the day.

Mo noticed that one of the vans sat outside the office all the time. It never went anywhere. Mo mentioned it to Corky and me, but was so buried in overdue bills that he did not follow up.

My Eggheads work kept me away from the office a couple of days longer than expected. The second Monday after deal completion, Mo stayed home and Corky became the one of us in the office.

The van was sitting in our car park because it wasn't roadworthy. Its brakes were shot. The steering was loose. The engine started with some coaxing, but sounded like it was at death's door. Two tyres had so little tread, they must have been illegal for a while.

Corky asked our office staff how that van had passed MOT. Toni said it hadn't. Vince and Pat used the van that was drivable, but both vans were due for MOT weeks earlier and neither had been through the inspection. How GLS got away with driving one of those vans every day when it was out of MOT, I don't know. There are cameras all over the country to look for such things as a vehicle registration plate on the road that doesn't match up with MOT and insurance records.

We got the better van through MOT with under £600 in repairs. By the time we had the sad van towed to a mechanic and repaired enough to pass MOT, the cost for both added up to about £2200. Mo chose to treat the episode as a single breach of the acquisition warranty that said all equipment was in good working order. Adding the costs to make both vans road-legal made a breach we could claim from Fanny.

Corky asked Toni whether road tax had lapsed for the vans, too. Most people and businesses renew MOT, road tax and insurance at about the same time. Not GLS. Road tax wasn't due again for a few months.

At the least, we should have put this on a checklist to go through as soon as acquisition occurred. It would have been better if we actually looked at the vans during our due diligence visit. MOT would still have expired after that visit, but we would have known what condition they were in. They didn't get so knackered overnight.

14 INSURANCE

Corky and I didn't have a commercial insurance broker. Mo did. With our agreement, he got his broker Edgar Goodman to look through all the GLS insurance coverage. Goodman found only a few minor gaps in standard coverage and no major policies lapsed. He recommended changing the fleet coverage at its next renewal date in a couple of months.

He also recommended Directors and Officers insurance, which GLS did not carry. Mo agreed, but said it would have to wait until our finances settled.

 In hindsight, not getting D&O coverage right away was a monumental mistake. Need I say more?

15 CORKY WRESTLES WITH ADVERTISING IN PRINT MEDIA

GLS needed a steady flow of high-quality leads. Office staff qualified leads over the phone before scheduling contracted sales representatives to visit potential customers. This meant sales representatives only got appointments with leads who looked able and eager to buy. When Varzen acquired control of GLS, Fanny claimed the reps were closing deals at 50% of their appointments. Corky dug into the figures with Kath, who managed them, and found the closing rate was really between 25% and 35%.

GLS advertised mostly in paper publications, especially in national media, and only a little online. Fanny targeted affluent pensioners for garden rooms and such, and she believed they didn't go online. Advertising in print media is expensive, especially at the national level where it costs a king's ransom. Cash flow falls apart if such costly marketing doesn't produce enough viable leads.

Kath said the reps really did close a deal at about every second appointment before the pandemic. These were the same reps, the same products, and what should be a hot market with everyone needing to spend so much more of their time at home. Having the close rate worsen this much indicated trouble deeper than getting a lower number of leads than before. The leads must be of weaker quality, too.

Did print media not perform well any more, or what?

Corky started looking more intensely at the adverts GLS was running.

When Mo resurrected the marketing, he raised the dead still in mummy wrappings. The adverts looked like they were from about 1980. They also had inconsistent branding and copy. They contained errors. One included a prominent photo of an installation team wearing another company's logo on their shirts.

Corky set up a virtual meeting with the solopreneur who designed the adverts so all three of us could meet him. Josh Singleton was so happy to see new management at GLS, he almost cried. We had been thinking we might need to get only the most immediate changes done by him for speed while we found a better designer to replace him. In the conversation, we learned that he had been hobbled by Fanny. She was unwilling to pay even a few pounds to modernise or even correct any adverts. He had been itching for years to do more for GLS.

Singleton and Corky immediately hit it off, feeding each other's enthusiasm for updated advertising with a fresh look and wider appeal. They made tentative plans. Within four days, Singleton delivered the most urgent corrections and minor tweaks. Then he inexplicably became unreachable.

We understood why when his obituary appeared about three weeks after our virtual meeting. At age 49, supposedly not at high risk, he got COVID and it killed him.

Before he died, Singleton made enough changes to get us started on a revamp of the print adverts. Corky turned to the agency that handled GLS' advertising placements in most of its print outlets and got their in-house designers to do a little more while he prepared for a full-throated refresh of the branding and advertising.

 We could have at least glimpsed adverts in print media ourselves by simply buying Sunday editions of certain national newspapers and a few regional publications during due diligence or at least before deal completion. The condition of the print marketing shouldn't have been a surprise to us.

16 CYBERSPACE IS NO BETTER

The second Thursday after deal completion, I joined Corky and the office staff at the office. While Corky dealt with marketing and sales, I took a look at the digital side of GLS. When I put into Google® any search term that should find our company, GLS only showed up in paid search results. No matter how I adjusted my search, it never showed up in free search results, and I don't just mean we didn't show up on the first page. We didn't show up, full stop.

The company had two different websites with inconsistent look and feel and content at gardenlivingspace.com, which was the primary site, and gardenlivingspace.co.uk.

Everyone's email was on gardenls.com. This was the super-secure server Peter set up in a corner of the office, which Fanny said no one could get into after Peter died.

Corky and I both dug into this, sometimes together and sometimes separately, whenever we could.

We found hints at what was going on in cached pages on the Web, but not enough to piece together the whole picture.

Corky contacted Cyber Simba Ltd, the IT service provider for GLS. Fanny relied on them for everything IT related. She was as averse to and ignorant about technology as her insistence on paper bills suggested. When they said the super-secure server couldn't be accessed, she believed them. When they said nothing about email at gardenls.com could be modified, she believed them. When they said office staff could only use email through a web browser, not an email client like Outlook®, she believed them.

First we got them to set up an email address of management@gardenlivingspace.com,
thinking we would move everyone to that domain and let them start using Outlook®. We quickly learned that email from our new address usually didn't get delivered. It was treated as spam. The domain was blacklisted for email.

We checked and found that its host had not been hacked. It was not spewing out spam campaigns. If it had, after we stopped the flood, the blacklists should have relented... but there was no flood to stop. Something else had flagged the domain so hard that we couldn't get it off the blacklists.

We pivoted. Corky started building a new website on gardenlivingspace.co.uk. He built it from scratch, as best he could, because we couldn't afford to hire a pro to do it for us. It didn't look great. We hadn't done anything about rebranding GLS yet. If we were going to switch to that as our main domain, we needed to settle the branding first.

But we could start a free trial of Microsoft 365® for GLS, set up email for everyone there using the .co.uk domain, and set up permission-controlled digital storage. Corky started the trial and we tested the waters with our own new email addresses on gardenlivingspace.co.uk. They worked.

We created email addresses for our employees and the sales reps. We moved Mo's folders for keeping track of bills into the new digital storage and set access controls on them. Together, Corky and I introduced the employees to all of this, and then had a virtual meeting with the sales reps to introduce their new email accounts. We helped everyone set up Outlook® as their email client. We showed the employees how to forward email from their gardenls.com accounts to their new accounts and set a deadline for copying all of it so we could decommission the clunky old email system.

We showed Toni how to file incoming bills in the Unpaid folder and how we would move them around as they got processed, at least until we had a proper accounting system that could store a copy of the bills with their entries into our books. We set up a folder structure and file naming convention to keep photos from customer jobs, which Kath would oversee.

The staff didn't quite understand about switching from a whiteboard to Outlook® calendars for scheduling customer fittings, sales rep visits, Vince and Pat, and so on. We decided to let them carry on with the whiteboard until they got accustomed to the new email, and then try online scheduling.

This felt like lots of progress, but we still couldn't get into the super-secure server.

 It didn't occur to anyone to establish acquisition warranties about any of this. We had nothing about domains being in compliance with Google's terms and conditions. We had nothing about the IT systems being fit for purpose and manageable. Worst of all, even if we had, we could only claim for specific costs of a warranty breach. It was impossible to distinguish the financial impact of not having full control of accounts, not appearing in search results unless we paid for it, and not having coherent, sensible IT.

Corky kept badgering Cyber Simba. We knew enough about IT to be able to push back at them. Our big breakthrough came when they admitted they knew a superuser login to the special server and another superuser login to administer gardenls.com. Corky dragged those logins out of them and we took a look at what was in there. I'm skipping over weeks of banging our heads against a brick wall. We got those logins about seven weeks after deal completion.

We did a lot of swearing after that.

17 SUPER-SECURE SERVER DISAPPOINTMENTS

Peter violated Google's terms and conditions, getting the main GLS domain blacklisted by Google®. That's why we only appeared in search results when we paid to appear. We found the files in the server. What he had done was convoluted, deliberate, saved a little bit of money at the time and had negative consequences forever. Fanny would not have understood it if she knew about it.

The email system really was so crude that it could only be accessed through a web browser. It held its data in a proprietary format and couldn't export email in a form that any other email system could import.

The super-secret server contained much of the older material we didn't get our hands on in due diligence. It had employment contracts, supplier contracts, the Cyber Simba service level agreement, and more.

It did not contain any nice tidy policy and procedure documents. It did not contain a nice tidy sales rep packet. The reason it didn't contain those was simple – they didn't exist. The server contained a hodgepodge of price lists that weren't even all done in the same manner (for example, some included VAT and some didn't), memoranda, and files about products in no particular order. We had paid a premium price for a business that supposedly had good, solid, extensive policies and procedures that had become unreachable due to Peter's death. We believed everyone was working to such procedures, and all of that could be documented again.

None of that had ever been cohesive and thoroughly put together.

 If a business cannot show clear, comprehensive documentation of its policies and procedures, only a fool believes it has good policies and procedures. We were Grade A fools.

18 PRICE LISTS AND SALES MATERIALS

Digging into money matters since our due diligence visit, cash flow didn't look right. We were selling at prices too low for our costs. Occasionally we sold at breakeven or at a slight loss. Sales reps had some latitude to negotiate around standard prices, within discounting guidelines. From what I saw, it was hard to figure out what the standard prices were. I asked Corky for the price lists.

Price lists had been in the disclosure bundle, but it was not clear how they fit together with each other or how old they were. Now we could see date stamps on them in digital folders. They ranged from a year and a half to three years old.

The pandemic on top of Brexit dramatically raised the costs of materials during the past three years. Some materials doubled in cost. A few went up even more. Despite that, GLS had not adjusted its prices at all.

Inexplicably, sales reps were half as effective at closing sales as they had been before, even though now they were offering bespoke garden rooms at what must be the bargain basement prices of the industry. Most of the sales reps had been on contract to GLS for years. Why was this happening?

Then we looked at the sales materials. Those were hopelessly behind the times, too, and chaotic. It was a wonder anybody sold anything for GLS at all.

We needed to update the sales kit, but making a better profit margin was more urgent.

Corky drew up new price lists, this time showing prices with and without VAT. The price increases were unavoidably large. If pricing had been adjusted on a regular basis, each step up would have been modest and in line with the cost increases driving it. Needing to make up to three years of adjustments in one leap was jarring at best.

The sales team collectively howled, saying it would be impossible to close any sales with the new pricing. They blamed new higher pricing for their low closing rates, even though the drop-off began before we revised price lists. Kath did what she could to calm them down, but some quit. The quitters tended to be the worst performers, so Corky and I weren't upset about losing them.

Lisa found a new sales rep. As soon as Kath onboarded her, Hannah started to develop her own sales materials and methods.

They worked. Her closing rate was better than anyone else's. She discounted less than anyone else, even with the challenge of our new higher pricing. She seemed to have an excellent feel for the market, and she wanted to start approaching a new demographic we had been discussing for expansion – professionals who needed to put an office in their garden. Now that the pandemic had made people work from home more, working at the kitchen table surrounded by restless children or in a conservatory that was usually too cold or too hot was clearly not tolerable for the long term.

We should be able to easily add to our catalogue of garden rooms, offering some products specifically intended to be comfortable as year-round office space.

 Why didn't we look at the sales kit during due diligence? Why didn't we compare supplier price lists with revenue?

19 BOTCHED FITTINGS

The acquisition warranties promised that no litigation was in progress or threatened and there were no unresolved customer complaints.

The third day Corky was in the office, Dick swung through briefly in the morning. When Corky asked what he would be doing that day, Dick said he was on the way to fix a problem at the Rutherfield garden room. Before Corky could get any details, Dick drove away.

Corky asked the office staff whether they knew anything about the Rutherfield job. Between them, Toni and Kath knew enough pieces of the story for Corky to get an outline.

The Rutherfields had a garden room and got it upgraded by GLS more than a year earlier. It was a premium job to install a new roof specially manufactured off-site. The roof was lightweight, looked more like a house roof than a garden room, had high grade insulation and included a built-in skylight. This was a top of the line product that greatly improved the look and interior comfort of a garden room.

The Rutherfield garden room was built into a corner of their garden. It wasn't a rectangle. It had a footprint more like a corner shed, as though the corner that would stick out into the garden the most had been lopped off. Usually that lopping-off is symmetrical, but in this case it wasn't. The sales rep sent inaccurate measurements, so what the factory made was off by a couple of centimetres here and there, and that made its angles wrong. The fitting team forced it on anyway. The roof kept developing leaks opened up by the resulting stresses.

Toni logged into the CRM to get figures for the job. Most of the cost to GLS had been the order for the factory-made roof. The profit margin would have been okay, but had been completely eaten by the cost of five site visits by Vince or Pat to patch leaks with sealant. The Rutherfields sent a letter a month before deal completion threatening legal action if GLS did not immediately and completely correct the problem. Now Dick was going back with more sealant to patch leaks again, and to persuade the Rutherfields not to sue.

 Our assumption that Fanny and Peter ran GLS as a team was wrong. He ran the company while she enjoyed its fruits and exercised her sales talent when she wanted. With only her at the top and

Dick as her lieutenant, it was not the business it had been. A couple of the customer complaints we discovered began while Peter was alive. Botched jobs and more serious failings escalated dramatically under Fanny and Dick, and were hidden from due diligence.

We were rattled. The pattern of repeated product failure was obvious, so we felt it should have been disclosed as an unresolved customer complaint. More importantly, although the legal threat came in after our due diligence visit, it occurred well ahead of deal completion. It was a clear breach of the warranties.

Dick held off the Rutherfields that day and made light of the situation when he got back to the office, but his sealant didn't hold any better than Vince's or Pat's. Two weeks later the Rutherfields called again, even more angry about having yet another leak and water-spotted ceiling. We could only resolve the complaint by ordering and fitting a replacement roof. It cost us over £6000 in materials and subcontracted labour.

I wish I could say this was a one-off. It wasn't. In fact, if we had looked more closely, we would have realised GLS fell short for the Rutherfields in another way they hadn't noticed yet, and that threatened even more harm to GLS than a mere claim for a few thousand pounds.

 In addition to the £100k of operating capital, we should have insisted on getting a set-aside fund for claims against the 10 year guarantee. As a standard feature of the company, a portion of the profit from every job should have gone into that reserve.

20 BANK WAS AN UNSAFE PLACE FOR MONEY

About three weeks after deal completion, the first bill for that expensive national advertising package had to be paid. This initial bill to restart services was higher than the remaining months should be, about £30,000. Corky paid it.

By this time, Corky and Mo had their own bank logins. Theirs were less powerful than mine, but able to see the current balance and latest transactions, and able to pay bills to existing suppliers.

Within hours after Corky paid that big bill, none of us could log in. We didn't know whether any customer payments were coming in or whether any automatic debits were going out. We didn't know what the balance was. We sent email to ask Fanny to take a look and she couldn't log in either.

As managing director, I called the bank. They kept me on hold half an hour, then told me that they could not speak with me because I was not the primary user on the account. I asked Fanny to call the bank. They kept her on hold even longer, then said they couldn't speak with her because she wasn't the primary user any more.

Each of the four of us kept calling the bank, sitting on hold for a long time and then trying to persuade a human at the other end of the telephone line to help us. With each call, one of us teased a little piece of inadvertent disclosure from customer service. Often the pieces were contradictory.

We were blocked because of the suspiciously large transaction. The large transaction had nothing to do with it. We were blocked because the bank mandate had not been processed yet, so Fanny was still the primary user and they could only talk with her. We were blocked because Fanny was no longer the primary user, but online access was never supposed to be granted before the bank mandate was processed, so it was our fault that we had taken their advice to do those steps out of order and set up a situation their systems could not handle. We were blocked because the identification steps each of us had been through were not recorded yet.

After three or four days of this, I got through to a woman in customer service who must have been working from home, probably due to the pandemic. We were going through the whole fraught story again when a very small child began screeching at full volume in the background. How many times have I been in a business call when one of my kids has done that? To get rid of me, she turned on my login access. I'm sure she wasn't supposed to do that, but it was enough to make it possible for me to manage the bills again.

During those few days, Fairweather got in touch with Mo to ask why his invoice was a week overdue. Fairweather had sent it promptly upon deal completion on Net 14 Days terms, as promised. We owed him about £25,000, thanks to him writing off a few grand in hope of getting our legal business for the future additional acquisitions we hoped to make. Mo filed it appropriately, but did not pay it during his days at the office. We were trying to bring and keep bills current, not pay bills early.

We discussed it in at least two of the management team meetings we held online. Corky promised to pay it a day or so ahead of the due date.

He hadn't paid it, and with the bank account frozen, now there was no way to pay it.

Mo was upset. We were stiffing his solicitor, so this could have repercussions for him. Corky apologised. Ever since completion day, we had been up to our ears in problems that were often surprises, direct violations of promises made in the purchase agreement. Overlooking a detail or two was understandable.

Unfortunately, we thought the bank account was now down to about £60k. If we paid the entire legal bill now, we could find ourselves unable to buy materials for an upcoming job or pay the fitting subcontractors, or payroll, or... something. It wasn't unusual for the bank balance to swing up or down by £30k or £40k in a single day. We also weren't sure whether the previous big outgoing payment had triggered our lockout from the bank account. Whenever we got into the bank account, we didn't want to risk getting shut out again.

Mo called Fairweather and, using the BMB situation as an excuse, persuaded him to allow us to split the bill into three payments made over the next three weeks. Corky said he would make the payments as soon as we resolved our BMB problem.

He made the first one, then forgot the next two. Fairweather contacted Mo when the second payment became slightly overdue. Mo in turn contacted Corky to get it done. When that happened again for the third payment, I think that's what prompted Mo to begin poking around, looking at what was happening to the extent that he could see it in files, and getting more involved in day to day operations than he was supposed to be.

We didn't recognise our personal strengths and weaknesses well enough. For example, Corky isn't good at detail and we stuck him with the detail work of overseeing all the bills. I was limiting my time working on GLS while I still had to work full time for Eggheads, so I expected Corky to take care of it until GLS was on its feet enough for me to drop Eggheads. I'm good at detail and should have taken care of that, or imposed on Mo to do it.

21 NO ACCOUNTING FOR THE ACCOUNTING

We got logins to use Max Minford's online accounting system. We had been looking forward to it, expecting it to tell us everything about GLS financial transactions up to the day of deal completion.

It looked okay up to about the time of our due diligence visit. After that, it was very incomplete.

It turned out that Fanny's procedure was to accumulate paper (bill printouts from Toni, bank statement printouts, receipts brought in by Dick, and so on). Once in a while, all that paper was mailed to Minford. Then it sat in Minford's offices for about three months before someone entered it into the online accounting system.

We had no idea what was awaiting data entry at Minford. They said they would get around to it in due course.

Mo, Corky and I each wandered around in the system. Bank account reconciliation had not been done in about three years. When we looked at the data, we found payments attributed to the wrong bills. We found transactions assigned to the wrong category.

We entered what we had processed since our acquisition. Corky began trying to use it to record bills and payments, and schedule reminders about bills that needed paying. But I wanted to use it to track cash flow. Beyond that, I wanted to build a cash flow projection model to help me manage our finances with some foresight and use the accounting system to feed the model. With gaping deficiencies in the data, the accounting system could not even approach anything as useful as perfectly ordinary, valid profit and loss statements.

 When we made our due diligence visit, Minford had just entered a batch of data. We noticed their fees were high, but it looked like the accounting reports were up to date and normal. We only looked at the reports. We didn't look at the system or ask how the financial information flowed.

Mo made arrangements for Franks to take over the accounting for GLS. Minford stonewalled. They wanted to do the filing for the financial year that finished at the end of last year. They needed to process the latest batch of paper into the system before they could do that. They would do everything in good time.

Nothing happened with Minford for a few weeks, despite repeated phone calls and emails from Franks and Mo. Eventually Minford said Fanny had not paid their last bill and in a week or so their next bill would be sent to us. If we paid everything GLS owed, they would begin the work they had promised.

Mo got them to send the overdue bill and the new bill. They were demanding more than £4k for doing nothing, as far as we could see. We had to pay it in order to have any chance of getting control of the accounting, ideally in time to meet the upcoming VAT filing date.

In the end, Mo had to get Franks to agree to handle the filing for the immediate past financial year as best she could with Minford's data. Then Mo put his foot down to demand the handover... and put it down again and again for more than a month before Franks was actually able to get her hands on the data and the last box of paperwork, which Minford had never even begun to enter into the system.

The data was so dirty, Franks never did get it cleaned up enough to import into her accounting system. But I'm getting ahead of myself in this sorry tale...

 The valuation of GLS that determined our acquisition price was based on unreliable accounting data. If we had insisted on the cutover to our accountant as part of the transaction, at least we would have learned right away how faulty the accounting data was. Then, if we had the right clauses in the purchase agreement (which we didn't), discovering the valuation was based on bad data could have given us a way to hand the business back to Fanny and recover our money right away.

22 CREDIT AND CASH FLOW CONTROL

Seeing what was happening to our cash flow and spooked by having our bank account frozen, Mo got two sets of cards for GLS. With his credit record, he had no difficulty doing that.

First, he got charge cards for Dick, Vince, Pat and Corky. These replaced the 'float' that Vince and Pat used for their expenses and Dick's casual attitude about expense reimbursements. It also took care of Corky.

Vince and Pat would tell Toni or Kath that they needed to replenish their float and they would get £500, no questions asked. They should have been submitting expense reports and receipts to document the business expenses paid for with that money, but GLS had no such thing as an expense report. At best, once in a while Dick tossed a handful of receipts on Toni's desk without explanation and left her to sort through them. I'm not sure Vince or Pat did even that much. Corky was working long days trying to get a handle on everything and didn't have time for lengthy reimbursement paperwork, but he needed reimbursement quickly.

Charge cards arrived and addressed all of that.

Vince and Pat no longer got expense advances. They used their charge cards to fuel the vans, buy supplies and so on. Their spending was now tracked. We still wanted receipts, if only to help support our VAT filings, but at least the spending was no longer freewheeling. We could now see Dick's spending within a day or so instead of only when he threw a handful of crumpled paper at Toni.

Corky no longer had to worry about juggling his money woes around his GLS expenses. He was beginning to do quite a bit of driving to visit customers with unresolved complaints. The fuel costs for those trips now went onto the GLS charge cards, and so did materials if he found the complaint was something he could readily fix himself while he was with the customer.

 The charge cards were one of our few good moves. They automatically paid themselves off by direct debit from the bank account every week, so they could not accumulate a big debt unless Corky used them for something unusually large. They did not require a personal guarantee. They made life easier for staff who worked some or all of the time away from the office, incurring business expenses nearly every workday. They allowed me to see what was happening with business expenses, transaction by transaction, almost immediately. I could import the transactions into accounting software or spreadsheets easily. The cards even gave us discounted prices on fuel for the vans and cars. There was no downside to them.

Mo didn't stop there. With more effort, he got credit cards for GLS. Mo, Corky and I had cards. Office staff had cards. Mo anticipated that we might hit the bottom of the bank account and need some access to credit, so this was intended as a safety cushion. We did need it, so for GLS maybe it was a good decision. For Mo, in the end it was a bad decision.

The credit card required a personal guarantee. Mo provided it. Corky and I couldn't have.

Getting ahead of myself again, toward the end we did go through the bottom of the bank account and needed some credit. Mo foresaw that accurately. We did not use the credit card the way we all agreed to use it. The first month, we paid it off in full. Then we began to carry a balance, telling ourselves that we would pay it off the next month when our cash position improved. The next month, our cash position was still precarious, so we carried the balance again, and it grew like a weed.

We put the fleet insurance renewal on it. We put online advertising costs on it. We put office stationery on it. We topped up the postage machine with it.

At one point, Mo tried setting a lower limit on how much each person could put on the card in one transaction, reducing it from low four digits to £500. Lisa was buying online advertising a thousand pounds at a time. Corky was having her try more and more advertising there in an effort to compensate for print media not producing anywhere near the leads it used to produce. Lisa and Corky said they each needed higher spending limits if we wanted to get any leads and make any sales, so Mo reluctantly raised Lisa's limit and took off Corky's.

 Mo wound up personally stuck with the credit card bill. What happened to Mo is exactly why everyone in M&A warns against signing any personal guarantees.

23 WHERE'S OUR DICK?

Although some of our woes were Fanny's doing, everything operational was within Dick's remit. We were increasingly perturbed by how much he was not managing. Instead, he was almost always out, driving around the country to redo the sales reps' site surveys and measurements for jobs, show up at suppliers in person to place special orders instead of sending them in by email or phone, redraw job sketches done by sales reps, make some of the sales visits himself, do repairs under the guarantee, and so on. He was our most expensive sales rep, small-job handyman, and supply clerk.

He wasn't providing guidance and supervision to the employees, or oversight to the contractors. When a problem cropped up at a fitting, he went and often insisted on working on it himself instead of coaching anyone about how to do their work better. We saw no hint of any effort to clean up the sales kit or keep an eye on the price lists or develop better processes, even though we told him to do that. He had let the vans become disreputable hulks and let their MOTs lapse.

Corky and I repeatedly told him what we expected of a General Manager and that he should be spending more time in the office. He carried on as though we said nothing. We usually didn't even know where he was or what he was doing.

He treated the rest of the employees like dirt, called them derogatory names, belittled Vince and Pat in front of subcontractors and customers at job sites... Small wonder the staff loathed him.

About a month after deal completion, Mo began saying in our virtual management meetings that we should not keep Dick. By then, we had sold one company car. Corky was shopping around for a plug-in electric hybrid as a new company car for Dick to drive so we could sell the current one and his Benefits In Kind tax could go down. Dick was the only reason to change the company car. Mo insisted we should reconsider whether to keep Dick before getting the hybrid car.

Corky and I were reluctant. Firing people is always awful. Besides, Dick was supposed to be one of the primary assets of the company.

A month and a half after deal completion, we had accumulated a list of about 10 unresolved customer complaints ranging from 2 months to

3 years old. These, too, indicated Dick was not doing his job as GM. The acquisition warranties promised none of this existed, but it did, and we were on the hook for it.

Corky went with Dick to see a couple of the garden rooms involved. One was botched because Dick had cut costs by overriding the subcontractors' recommendation about how to do a tricky portion of it, and the cheaper approach left an unusual garden room that was not sturdy enough.

Also at the month and a half mark, Dick went to a job site, berated Pat in front of a subcontractor crew at a customer site, and went so far that Pat blew his top.

We started a formal management investigation. That seemed to take both men by surprise. The subcontractors heard it all, but weren't in line of sight and didn't see whether punches were thrown. Pat and Dick each said the other had swung a punch and each swore to have walked away. It quickly became clear that both had, at best, behaved like bratty boys instead of mature adults. Dick didn't understand why we believed it was more his responsibility than Pat's. Dick was a boss and should de-escalate troublesome situations, not escalate them.

Our investigation began to pull loose threads that led to other concerns. Dick had verbally threatened Vince and Pat on multiple occasions. Dick had been arrested three times for violent assaults, and somehow escaped conviction each time. He bragged about that at local pubs. We found more, but this was enough.

This time, when Mo said we should fire Dick, Corky and I agreed.

We contracted with a human relations company to help us do it properly. We had begun to understand that we needed not to leave Dick any latitude about it, but as the only hire after Peter's death, Dick was the only employee with an actual employment contract and it required 4 weeks notice. The HR company helped us write the termination letter to put Dick on garden leave through his notice period (during which he was not to visit the office, not to do work for GLS and not to work for anyone else). The HR firm determined exactly what steps to do in which order, and we decided who should do each part.

Termination needed to be done by a director, so Corky couldn't do it. We needed to allow an avenue for Dick to file an internal appeal, so as managing director I shouldn't do it. That left Mo stuck with the task of actually firing Dick. Corky would be in the room too as a witness and in case Dick got violent. We would do it on a Friday afternoon so nobody would be in the office again until after Dick had a couple of days to cool off. We would send him home in a taxi and keep the company car so that when he left the building, we would have all the company items he had been using.

The big day was the first time Mo returned to the office. I was off-site, as planned. If I had anything to do with the termination meeting, I couldn't handle an appeal. When the staff showed up, Mo asked Toni to arrange a taxi to pick him up at 2 o'clock for a 20 mile trip on the company's tab. Mo said his car had barely gotten to the office and he needed to get to an appointment at a supplier in the afternoon. It was weird. The staff understood something must be happening. Nobody knew what it was, so everyone was jittery.

Dick was late for the meeting Corky had scheduled with him. Once he got there, Mo took him into one of the office rooms and went through the process as planned. Mo recorded audio of the termination meeting, which he told Dick he was doing up front. After the meeting, Mo sent a copy of the recording to Dick's personal email address.

The only hitch was that Dick pitched a fit over losing his company car. He and his wife each had a personal car, but in the meeting Dick said his car wasn't running. Without the company car, he would be stranded. His employment contract said he got a company car and he was determined to keep it until the end of his notice period.

Dick treated the car roughly already. If he kept it, he might easily sabotage it. With all the overdue bills and customer disputes draining our cash, we needed to sell the car for as much as we could get.

Coming up with a solution on the fly, Mo said the contract promised a company car, not necessarily the one Dick drove now. Mo promised to rent a car for Dick to use for 4 weeks and have it delivered to his home the next morning.

Corky supervised Dick's packing of any personal items in his office and ushered him out to the taxi while Mo met with the rest of the office staff in another room to tell them what we had just done. He said later that none of them did a good job of hiding their delight. I could swear I heard some whoops of joy all the way over at my house when the office day ended.

It took Mo a couple of hours to arrange the car rental. It was a Vauxhall Corsa, a type of car Dick would regard as beneath his status, on a flat rate with unlimited mileage allowance, for delivery to Dick's home in the morning. GLS prepaid but the contract was Dick's, and so was responsibility for the condition of the car when he returned it.

In three more months, Dick would have reached his second anniversary as an employee at GLS. After that, employment law would have made it a lot harder to get rid of him.

 Getting advice from specialists to help us handle the termination properly was a good decision. Dick tried to find ways to fight it, but we had not left any gaps for him to use to file an appeal against or take to an employment tribunal. We should have done it sooner.

Corky started going through Dick's office. He found a letter from a customer threatening legal action over a botched garden room. In the next couple of workdays, Corky and I went through every bit of that office. We found a couple more threats of legal action from other customers, one of whom wasn't in our list of unresolved disputes yet. We found paper bills from suppliers we hadn't heard of before and hadn't seen payments for in the bank statements.

We found building regulations approval for a premium garden room. That caught our attention.

 We should have done a formal, in-depth evaluation of every employee at the start and fired anyone we didn't want to keep. That would have nipped trouble in the bud. But to recognise Dick as a problem right away, we would have needed to exercise our power as bosses to go through everyone's desk after hours. We were too nice to do that.

24 MARKETING FALLING FLAT

We were only a couple of months into revived marketing, not quite long enough to see the full effect, but Lisa could see a pattern emerging. Advertising in print no longer performed the way it used to. The market shifted in the pandemic. Demand for GLS' products was enhanced by the pandemic, but local and regional print media now performed better than national media and online might be able to outperform all print media.

In the evenings after my work for Eggheads, I sifted through GLS data as best I could and saw that she was right. We had poured our precious money into the most expensive marketing channels, which were now the worst performing channels. We had to pivot.

 If we had required Fanny to continue operating the company normally all the way up to our acquisition, we would have been able to see that national print marketing was no longer worthwhile. Instead, she was able to shut it all down and leave us with only past history to go by, hiding crucial information about shifts in the market that we needed in order to survive.

25 POTENTIALLY UNLIMITED LIABILITY

Fanny never mentioned needing building regulations approval or planning permission for any of the bespoke garden rooms that GLS built or upgraded. I thought sheds, summerhouses and garden rooms didn't need any of that. Finding a BR approval in Dick's desk made me wonder whether we were missing something.

Oh, were we ever missing something!

When we asked Kath about it, she didn't remember anything about it. Nothing about it was in the CRM, either. Dick apparently arranged for the approval himself without telling anyone or putting it into the CRM. Corky, Kath, Toni, Lisa and I all clustered together to look through the photographs from that fitting. It quickly became obvious that the images Dick submitted to get the approval came from somewhere else. It wasn't the same outbuilding at all.

We looked up the UK government's published rules about outbuildings. To our shock, we realised that although GLS garden rooms were unlikely to need planning permission, some of them did require BR approval, mostly in the past three years when GLS began taking on more ambitious orders for a more affluent clientele. The approval was little more than a rubberstamp exercise with local Building Control. Getting through it cost about £300 in expenses and official fees.

If it was required and was not done within a grace period of a couple of years, we were liable for fines levied by the local government authority, and there was no limit on the size of the fines, *per instance.*

From the government website, we made a list of the criteria that would require BR approval, such as floor area above 30 square metres, or inclusion of sleeping accommodations (even a bunk for naps counted), or siting within one metre of the property boundary when the materials were combustible. Toni and Kath scoured the CRM looking for previous orders that needed BR approval.

They found 34. The only one with any evidence of having approval was the one documented in Dick's office, and that approval had been obtained with falsified evidence. The fact that one approval had been obtained showed us that

Dick and Fanny knew approvals were sometimes needed. Not getting approvals was a deliberate choice.

 Everything about breaches of acquisition warranties was written in terms of money. Claims about breaches had to be filed in terms of cost and could only be remediated by reimbursement of the cost. If a breach didn't incur a specific, readily documented cost, no claim could be filed about it. Technically, we could not claim the missing BR approvals as a breach until we either had to pay to retrospectively obtain the approvals or pay fines due to not having the approvals. If they were treated as separate instances, they would only be large enough to claim after fines were levied.

In our acquisition breach spreadsheet, Mo treated all of the missing BR approvals as one claim due to the obvious pattern of routinely ignoring regulatory requirements. He based the claim on the cost Corky and I calculated for retrospectively getting the missing approvals issued.

26 TRAPPED IN AMBER

Cash was low. We transferred into GLS nearly all of the money we still had in Varzan to get it through its cash squeeze, which we believed was temporary.

Mo had begun sending Fanny letters of claim for acquisition warranty breaches, accompanied by his tracker. If she paid even just the portion of the claims that we had already spent on trouble she warranted we wouldn't face, it could get us through our cash squeeze. Resolving each customer complaint she left us with had cost us anywhere from £250 to £15,000. That big one really hurt, and there were a couple of others that had already cost between £5k and £10k each.

The purchase agreement only required us to send notice through email. Fanny ignored it.

Mo sent the second update by email and as hardcopy by International Signed For air mail. It took three weeks to reach France, then terminated with a note that it was undeliverable due to an invalid postal address. He double checked the address he had used against the legal notice address she had put in the purchase agreement. He had sent it to that address.

In one of our virtual management meetings, together we searched for her actual street address. Corky found her in social media and eventually dug up some photos she posted of her French house there. I used Google® Street View to virtually drive up and down streets in the vicinity of her notice address, working my way outward in a spiral while all three of us looked for anything that resembled the social media images. Eventually, more than a mile from her stated address, we found the house.

Mo sent hardcopy again, this time by a private courier company, to the house we had found online. It got delivered. We had her signature to confirm that. We still got no response.

 If there had been a reserve against warranty breaches, we could have dealt with the solicitor managing that reserve. Instead, we had to wring money directly out of Fanny, who could simply ignore us... and as our experience with the bank mandate suggested, by taking the money to France she had effectively taken it beyond our reach.

Like many boys, when I was growing up I went through a phase where I was fascinated with bugs. Other boys pinned insects to a board for their collections. I sought insects trapped in lumps of amber. I found them at shops full of peculiar old cast-offs, places my mum called 'rubbish shops'. What was it like for those insects when they got stuck there? How could they have been entombed without any visible appearance of panic or thrashing?

We were now trapped in amber.

Even though Fanny's 30% of the shares were non-voting, the shareholder agreement gave her a form of veto power. Her consent was required for us to alter our ownership of GLS, or restructure the company, or drop a product line, or branch out into an adjacent industry, or close the business. We could only close the company without her consent if it was insolvent.

Corky, Mo and I were all trapped in our ownership of the company. Mo was trapped in his post as a director. I was trapped as managing director.

We faced potentially unlimited liability for the missing building regulations approvals. We could not escape by closing the company. We had not bought Directors and Owners insurance coverage, which might have covered some of our liability exposure, and now we were in too deeply and knew too much to be able to buy it.

 The legals for the deal should have allowed us to void the transaction, handing the company back to Fanny and getting our money back from her, if any breach of an acquisition warranty was too severe to tolerate.

27 OVERDUE BILLS THAT WERE OUR FAULT

As the end of Dick's termination notice period approached, we thought we got a grip on the existential crisis we had found in his desk. Corky negotiated arrangements with a company that specialised in handling building regulations approvals like what we needed. Getting them to agree to do ours retrospectively took some of Corky's best persuasion skills. He and I laid out a schedule to get them done over the span of about six months, spreading the costs.

There was no way we could absorb that much right now. We were so close to the bottom of the bank account, we couldn't even begin yet. We needed to ramp up sales. Going into the summer high season, surely we could do that, and then our cash squeeze would relent.

 Mo called Fairweather to ask whether he was doing what he needed to do to collect from Fanny for breaches of acquisition warranties. Fairweather said he was doing the right things for the time being. If Fanny didn't pay, the next step would be legal action. In the post-Brexit legal landscape, that might or might not succeed. Even if it did, it wouldn't be worth the solicitors' fees unless the amount being claimed was over £200k. We had to proceed on the assumption that warranty breaches were total losses. Our minimum possible cost of getting past them added up to nearly £100k, if pigs flew and unicorns pranced through the office, and we were well on our way into that morass.

Demand for GLS' products was enhanced by the pandemic, but local and regional print media now performed better than national media and online might be able to outperform all print media. Corky was shifting our advertising accordingly.

Meanwhile, Mo remembered what happened with Fairweather's bill. As the dust began to settle from Dick's termination and the building regulations crisis, Mo began spot-checking bills in the bill folders against bank statements. The accounting system was hopelessly out of date, so there was no point in checking there. All entries into it had stopped while we waited for accountancy to fully transfer into Franks' system. Minford was stalling that transfer.

The first of our big monthly bills for national advertising had been paid. Mo was still in the office paying bills when that one came in. They had demanded payment up front before they would begin placing adverts.

No transaction showed up at the bank to pay the second. Mo raised that as an issue in our virtual management meeting. Corky admitted he must have gotten sidetracked before actually setting up the payment for it.

We didn't have enough cash to pay a bill of that size unless we stiffed our subcontractors or missed payroll, and we certainly couldn't do either of those. Before deciding what to do, we checked the status of all our bills from that agency.

There had been three so far. Only the first had been paid. The other two were both overdue. It was a £50k hole, not £25k.

Mo said we should consider whether we were still solvent. I pulled up the mathematical model I had built for our cash flow projections. It wasn't what I hoped to build eventually, and I had to fill in all the data manually instead of pulling it from the accounting system, but it did enough. Corky fed me a series of what-if ideas until we found a way to make it all turn out okay. Corky only had to negotiate a payment plan with the agency that fit the scenario we had just modelled. He succeeded.

Then I got a call from the regional and local advertising agency. We were behind on their bills, too. Could we please bring our account with them up to date? If we didn't pay their bills on time, they had to pay the media outlets out of their own pockets and they were too small to survive much of that.

Hard on the heels of that call, I got a letter from HMRC. Fanny had not paid two rounds of employer's taxes the previous year, which were now accruing interest and penalties. This was yet another breach of an acquisition warranty. To add insult to injury, we had only paid the employers' taxes for the first round of payroll after deal completion. Mo made that payment. After that, we dumped all the bill handling and payments on Corky and he missed the next two tax payments.

 We expected Corky to keep track of bills and payments when that type of detail was a weak spot. We did not set up any formal mechanism to check each other's work until we at least got the business running the way we wanted it. If Mo had not looked at the bills and payments, we would have been completely blindsided and our shutdown would have been even more graceless than it was.

28 OVER THE EDGE

Once again, we needed a specialist and Mo knew one. We called Clarity Black, an insolvency practitioner and liquidator. Mo had considered acquiring a collapsed company that she handled. Although he didn't put in a bid, he was impressed by how creative and determined she was about trying to salvage whatever was most valuable about the company. Mo knew other insolvency practitioners, but she stood out. If we could avoid going under, she could tell us how.

We held a virtual meeting with her. We laid out our situation. I showed our now-dismal cash flow projections.

She was blunt, saying 'You need to close this business right now.' Then she added, 'By the way, your acquisition transaction was illegal.'

What?

After more discussion, she decided we should limp along another week in order to make one last round of payroll and then immediately terminate all our staff. It would be more kind to the employees. If we didn't do that, each employee could only get £800 in their last pay. They would have to put in a claim to the government for a statutory top-up, which wouldn't cover the entire gap in their pay. In normal times, that top-up would take six weeks to come through. Now, with pandemic delays, it would take months.

Black would handle liquidation of GLS. All our creditors were unsecured, so they were all on the same footing, with only one having a personal guarantee. Whatever cash she could raise by selling the company's assets would be divided among the creditors on a proportionate basis. Usually they would get 20% to 80% of what they were owed, after however many months it took to wrap up everything.

When we realised we were going under, we owed more than £15k on the credit card. In a panic, Corky used the card to buy more than £5k of advertising for GLS a couple of days before we met with Black. Mo hit the roof. It was a complete waste, placing adverts for a company being abruptly shut down, and it was going to come out of his personal wallet. He hammered on both of us until I paid enough from the bank into the card to bring it back down to where it had been. This left the bank account too thin to cover our final payroll, but I bit my tongue about that in the meeting with Black.

We could make payroll for everyone except Corky and me. The two of us would only get a fraction of our normal pay. That seemed fair. GLS had never been able to pay dividends after the acquisition. Mo wasn't on payroll at all, so the only money he ever got from the acquisition was petty reimbursement of expenses for going to the office a couple of times. Corky and I at least got a couple of paychecks before it all fell apart. Complaining about a short final paycheck would have been unseemly.

As for the acquisition transaction, its structure was a money laundering scheme. CBILS money was supposed to be used to sustain or grow the business, which the loan agreement clearly stated. It was not meant to line the personal pockets of the owners. Minford's deal structure laundered the CBILS money through Varzan and into Fanny's hands. It was illegal for her to take the CBILS money for herself and we helped her do it.

I wonder whether if it had gone directly into her personal account without going through Varzan, BMB might have caught on to what was happening and blocked it.

 A self-funded acquisition is every M&A person's dream. We had one. It seemed too good to be true, and it was.

29 WHERE ARE WE NOW?

During the week before GLS formally went into liquidation, we had a virtual meeting with Fairweather. We explicitly said we were not asking for any services and could not pay for the session, but thought he would want to know what was happening in case any consequences come through to him. As he listened to our outline of events at GLS, his jaw fell open. The only remark he made during the story was a squeak about the money laundering. About that, he said he's a solicitor, not a finance person, so he was relying on Minford's advice.

When we finished and asked whether he had any questions, it took him a moment to find his voice. He said that in 22 years as a solicitor, and as a partner in his firm, he had never heard of anything close to our situation.

He didn't try to offer any advice. He thanked us for the heads-up.

We should not have used a solicitor one of us knew to be good with business matters. We should have found a solicitor who specialises in mergers and acquisitions. I'm sure our situation does not look unique to M&A sharks.

Legally, Varzan owes GLS all the money it borrowed from GLS to fund the acquisition. Black's solicitor sent us a letter demanding that money from Varzan. We can't pay it. Varzan has to start making payments on its own CBILS loan soon, but all its cash went into attempting to bail out GLS. We sent good money in with doomed money.

Mo insisted that we hire a solicitor of our own to respond to the demand. It had to be a new one he found. We can't use a solicitor who was involved in the acquisition.

Our message is the same whether we say it or a solicitor says it for us. We're tapped out. It's just that the solicitor knows how to say it properly and give us the best possible chance of Black moving on to seek money elsewhere.

Mo had to pay for the solicitor. He doesn't have children to feed, just a now-angry wife.

I'm trying to keep Eggheads very happy so they will keep me and continue to pay me enough to feed and shelter my family.

In theory, if Black can't get money from Varzan or from us personnally, she can seek it from anyone who has been a director in the past four years – excluding Peter, of course, because he's dead. Unfortunately, Brexit didn't only mess up bank mandates across the border between the UK and EU. As long as Fanny is in France, there is no longer a straightforward legal path to go after Fanny for her illegal use of a big CBILS loan. Black is obligated to try, but expects to fail.

After that, she can try to seize any assets Fanny still owns in the UK or nab Fanny during visits here. That holds better possibilities, but I'm not holding my breath. It looks to me like Fanny has abandoned her plans to visit family in the UK from time to time. I wouldn't be surprised if she is quickly selling anything she owns here and spiriting the money across the Channel before Black can grab it.

The credit card company was not willing to abide by the usual rules for insolvency. They threatened to turn Mo over to a collections agency right away, adding thousands in penalties and fees to the bill. They continued to accrue interest on the balance. Mo liquidated some of his retirement savings to begin payments on the bill. Every payment he makes reduces the amount that might eventually be defrayed by the liquidator. Each payment is a complete loss to him.

So far, Mo and I are still on speaking terms. Corky went quiet. Once in a while I have to drag some information out of him, but he was not a director so he is not directly threatened by the collapse. He's trying to rebuild his life. I miss my bestie but I don't know how to get our rapport back. Mo and I wish we could rebuild our lives, but we still don't know whether Black will come around again to see whether there is any way to squeeze more out of us.

Mo and I also don't know whether we will have to go to court about being part of a money laundering scheme. From what Black tells us, the professionals involved in putting the deal together will get no more than a slap on the wrist, which their insurance will cover. All the responsibility is ours. We were supposed to know better even if the accountants and lawyers didn't.

 The gurus say you can become a millionaire in as little as three years by acquiring businesses. Or you could be like us. Good luck.

Printed in Great Britain
by Amazon